I0137335

Lessons From Bible Characters

By
Commander Michael H. Imhof
United States Navy

World rights reserved. This book or any portion thereof may not be copied or reproduced in any form or manner whatever, except as provided by law, without the written permission of the publisher, except by a reviewer who may quote brief passages in a review.

The author assumes full responsibility for the accuracy of all facts and quotations as cited in this book. The opinions expressed in this book are the author's personal views and interpretations, and do not necessarily reflect those of the publisher.

This book is provided with the understanding that the publisher is not engaged in giving spiritual, legal, medical, or other professional advice. If authoritative advice is needed, the reader should seek the counsel of a competent professional.

Copyright © 1994 Michael H. Imhof
ISBN-13: 978-1-57258-019-0 (Paperback)
Library of Congress Control Number: 94-61442

Scripture taken from the New American Standard Bible, © 1960, 1962, 1963, 1968, 1971, 1972, 1973, 1975, 1977 by the Lockman Foundation. Used by permission.

Contents

Introduction

The Bible is full of wisdom. It provides God's plan of salvation and promises for victorious living. It continually teaches us with the Holy Spirit's assistance as we read and study it. No matter what book you look into, you'll see the Bible has wisdom for everyday living.

The purpose of this book is to examine 35 situations where we can learn from Bible characters. Believe me, there are many more. I've basically presented short summaries of the situations and draw analogies and simple conclusions for everyday living. I've learned from my military endeavors and life to try and keep things simple and easily understandable.

I pray this book will be a blessing for you. I pray you'll be able to apply these simple lessons to your life.

1

David And Goliath

Several principles for military training and normal civilian life can be observed when analyzing the story of David and Goliath. David, a shepherd's boy, departed his father's flock to take grain and loaves of bread to his brothers who were gathered at the valley of Elah near Jerusalem. The Israelites were set to do battle with the Philistines. For 40 days Goliath, the Philistine champion who was well over nine feet tall, came out and taunted the army of the Israelites. Every time Goliath came forward, the Israelites cowered in fear behind their line of defense. On the morning David arrived, he heard Goliath's taunting and faith steered in his heart to go and face this Philistine. Why would a teenage shepherd's boy go out and do battle with a giant when the men of Israel were fearful for their lives?

First, David had an inner conviction in his spirit that he would overcome this obstacle. He stated to King Saul that the Lord had delivered him from the paw of the lion and bear and that He would do the same with this Philistine. An interesting parallel would be that when David killed both a lion and bear on different occasions to protect his father's flock that God had him in preparation. Equally, military units must train in a realistic manner and successfully prepare in peacetime for the later battle. Successful preparation, individually and corporately, breeds later success.

David's prior preparation and inner conviction drove out fear and developed confidence. Fear, the opposite of faith, causes torment and must be eliminated or it will affect one's performance in an adverse way. We see this with the army of Israel as they cowered in fear while David had an inner conviction of faith that he would triumph.

Secondly, David refused King Saul's armor saying he had not tested it. He shook it off and took his staff and five smooth stones to the battlefield. He had tested these throughout his life and had confidence in their use. He was proficient and ready for this challenge. Equally, military units must use and gain confidence in their weapons of war during peacetime in order to be proficient and ready for the later battle.

Thirdly, David refused to accept the negative comments from the others that said he was not able, that he was only a boy while Goliath a mighty warrior. I highlight this point to focus on the spirit. Negative comments, if one is not careful, will affect one's spirit and thinking. You'll notice that David's comments and corresponding actions consistently demonstrated David's belief and trust in the Lord for victory. David guarded his heart in this situation. If he had not guarded his heart and maintained his steadfast confidence in God, fear and subsequent defeat would have come. One is never defeated in life as long as one's spirit is not defeated for the spirit is capable of dominating the flesh.

2
Choose The Better Course

Absalom had just plotted the murder of Amnon. He had waited until the appropriate time to avenge Amnon's rape of his sister Tamar. The time had come and Absalom's servants carried out his orders just as he planned. Upon fruition, Absalom fled from Jerusalem and went to Geshur. King David gradually accepted the fact of Amnon's death and became anxious to see Absalom after he had been in exile for three years. Eventually, through a subtle plan of Joab, Absalom was able to return to Jerusalem and ultimately restored to King David's favor and full court privileges.

However, things were not the same as before. Absalom, during his time of separation from his father, had grown bitter. He meticulously plotted to usurp King David's throne by creating dissatisfaction among the people and promising good things to the people if they would make him king. Absalom proceeded to gain popular support and forced King David to flee Jerusalem for his life. God then used Hushai, David's spy and loyal friend, to lead Absalom into a snare. Hushai's counsel bought David time and flattered Absalom into taking personal command of the pursuit of David. The battle took place in the treacherous forest of Ephraim where Joab slayed Absalom.

Absalom's bitterness had grown into rebellion. This, coupled with pride, created a pursuit of power. Roots of bitterness have driven many people toward evil deeds. Absalom's bitterness affected a kingdom and thus it is in many lives. That's how it is with bitterness. One who retains bitterness will negatively affect oneself and the lives of many others. Tyrants and evil leaders spurred by bitterness have done it throughout time and so have common folks.

One may recall seeds of bitterness were planted in a defeated Germany shortly after World War I over a perceived unfair Treaty of Versailles. This helped lay the foundation for a man by the name of Adolph Hitler to seize power and lead the world into a war that destroyed millions of lives. Seeds of bitterness have further generated the organization and cruel retaliation acts of terrorist organizations throughout the world over religious differences and perceived wrongs. The list goes on.

Bitterness is a harsh companion for anyone and its fruits destroy wherever it is nurtured. Forgive and let bitterness go. This is truly the better course. "See to it that no one comes short of the grace of God; that no root of bitterness springing up causes trouble, and by it many be defiled." (Hebrews 12:15).

3
Learn To Forgive

A father had two sons. The younger son asked for his share of the estate and left for a distant land where he squandered his wealth on loose living. A famine occurred in the land and the man came into great need. He found himself feeding swine and suffering hunger. Remembering that his father had hired men that ate better than him, the young man decided to return to his father and ask for his forgiveness.

Upon return, the son approached his father with a humble attitude. His father immediately had the best robe and sandals brought out for his son. He ordered that the fattened calf be slain and that a celebration begin. The father's son had gone astray but now had returned. Music and dancing proclaimed the father's great joy and pleasure.

The experience of this relationship can be so easily compared to salvation. Our Heavenly Father looks down upon those who have gone astray from Him with much compassion. He rejoices and meets sinners with open arms when they return. There's rejoicing in Heaven over the salvation of one sinner. Our Heavenly Father is a good God and does not hold grudges toward any man or woman. There is no common sin big or wide enough that is not covered by the blood of Jesus. God forgives and loves with a wonderful love. It greatly pleases Him to see one sinner return to Him. He's more than willing to pour out blessings upon all who will receive Him.

Many family relationships today are torn apart because of unforgiveness, grudges and bitterness. Children are bitter toward their parents and parents bitter towards their children. Many people will live much of their lives not talking to family members or friends who they believe have offended them. Family relationships and friendships need not be this way. A domestic dog when harmed by its owner will often lick the hand of the individual that harmed him right afterwards. This type of action typically melts the owner. "Let all bitterness and wrath and anger and clamor and slander be put away from you, along with all malice. And be kind to one another, tenderhearted, forgiving each other, just as God in Christ also has forgiven you." (Ephesians 4:31–32). Learn to forgive. It may seem hard to do but it sets the path towards inner healing and restoration of relationships.

4
Heart Of Appreciation

Mary Magdalene was a solemn appearance on Easter morning. She was standing outside the tomb of Jesus and weeping when she stooped and looked in. She beheld two angels in white sitting at the head and feet of the area where Jesus had been placed. The discourse from that point is exceptionally impressive because she was to have a discussion with the risen Savior. During that discussion Jesus had to stop her from clinging to Him for He had not yet ascended to the Father.

Think of this situation. Jesus appeared first to Mary Magdalene in whom He had previously cast out seven devils. It was not Peter, James, John or even his mother that He gave this honor. Mary Magdalene loved Jesus deeply and appreciated Him so much. He had done much for her, rescuing her from a wicked life of prostitution to a life of hope and repentance. Mary Magdalene had such a heart of appreciation and let it be said that no depth of sin or possession of devils will separate us from the love of God as demonstrated in her life. She recognized Christ's love and treasured it deeply.

The resurrection is crucial to the Christian's faith. Through the resurrection of Jesus, mankind was once again linked back to the Father. It is interesting to note that when Jesus appeared to Mary Magdalene that He had not yet presented Himself and His blood before the Father. In this great plan of redemption, Jesus took time en route to the Father to appear to a Hebrew woman that was formerly a great sinner. Mary Magdalene's heart of appreciation to the Master would not be quenched and Jesus honored it greatly.

Imagine going up on the top of a mountain and looking in all directions. You would be impressed with the vastness of the area you could take in with your eyes. Now compare that to God's love and realize you're right in the middle of it. "For I am convinced that neither death, nor life, nor angels, nor principalities, nor things present, nor things to come, nor powers, nor height, nor depth, nor any other created thing, shall be able to separate us from the love of God, which is in Christ Jesus." (Romans 8:38–39).

Let us also have hearts of appreciation for all He has done for us. "But God demonstrates His own love toward us, in that while we were yet sinners, Christ died for us." (Romans 5:8). "Every good thing bestowed and every perfect gift is from above, coming down from the Father of lights, with whom there is no variation, or shifting shadow." (James 1:17).

5
Man Of Integrity

Abner brought David to Saul shortly after David slew Goliath in the Valley of Elah. Now it came about when David had finished speaking to Saul, that the soul of Jonathan, Saul's son, was knit to the soul of David, and Jonathan loved him as himself. Jonathan then proceeded to make a covenant with David and stripped himself of his robe and gave it to David with his armor, sword, bow and belt. Jonathan's commitment to David would later be tested.

Saul's attitude towards David grew progressively worse. Saul sought to put David to death since he was jealous of David and perceived him as the Lord's anointed. David prospered in all his endeavors. Eventually, David fled from Naioth in Ramah, and came and said to Jonathan, "What have I done? What is my iniquity? And what is my sin before your father, that he is seeking my life?" (I Samuel 20:1). Jonathan attempted to dismiss David's concern; however, David was sure Saul meant him harm. Thus, Jonathan went back and by carefully observing the actions of his father, Jonathan knew that Saul had decided to put David to death. Jonathan left to warn David of this impending danger through a prearranged signal involving three arrows. Jonathan grieved over his father's attitude and sent David safely away after they wept together.

Jonathan honored his commitment to David even in the face of opposition to his father. Jonathan had to take a stand against Saul's unrighteous anger for he knew his father was wrong in his actions towards David. Jonathan's integrity would not allow him to break his commitment to David when he could easily have done so.

Saul perceived David to be a threat to the throne and if Saul killed David, then in reality, Jonathan would surely succeed him as king. A man of integrity will always keep his word even when it costs him something. Jonathan refused to inherit the throne in this manner. "He who walks in integrity walks securely, But he who perverts his ways will be found out." (Proverbs 10:9). "The integrity of the upright will guide them, But the falseness of the treacherous will destroy them." (Proverbs 11:3).

6

An Able Man

The Pharaoh's daughter went down to the Nile to bathe and saw a basket along the river bank. She opened it and saw a Hebrew baby. The Pharaoh's daughter took the child as her son and named him Moses. Little did she know the hand of God was on this child.

Moses grew up in Egypt watching the Hebrew people do hard labor under the Egyptians. One day, out of sympathy, he killed an Egyptian who was beating a Hebrew and hid him in the sand. When Pharaoh heard of this, he tried to kill Moses but Moses fled to Midian. Moses then married Zipporah and stayed in this land while the Israelites continued to groan in their slavery under the Egyptians.

Moses, now away from Egypt, was about to be reached by God for a special work. He was tending the flock of his father-in-law, Jethro, when the Angel of the Lord appeared to him in flames of fire from within a bush on Mt. Horeb. Moses saw, that though the bush was on fire, it did not burn up. God called Moses from the burning bush and told him he had a work for him. The Lord said He had seen the misery of the Israelites under the Egyptian bondage and was sending Moses to Pharaoh to bring the Israelites out of Egypt. Moses immediately responded "Who am I, that I should go to Pharaoh and bring the Israelites out of Egypt?" (Exodus 4). Their discussion continued with Moses coming up with different excuses on why he wasn't able even though God said he would be with him. Moses pleaded with God to send someone else. Eventually, Moses became obedient and returned to Egypt. Ultimately, with God's help, Moses led the Israelites out of Egypt and the rest is Judeo-Christian history.

So many times people do not believe they're capable of certain tasks or assignments. Lack of confidence or experience affect their thinking and causes them to shrink back from pursuit of accomplishment and success. Let's look at Moses. He gave the Lord numerous excuses why it wasn't good to send him. Let's learn from this. As we develop our relationship with the Lord, we need to understand that He's there to help us. We need to go forth in the face of challenges with diligence and perseverance. As we do our part, look for God to do His. He helped Moses, and not being a respecter of persons, He'll help us. "Do not fear, for I am with you; Do not anxiously look about you, for I am your God. I will strengthen you, surely I will help you, surely I will uphold you with My righteous right hand." (Isaiah 41:10). "I can do all things through Him who strengthens me." (Philippians 4:13).

7
Courage To Change

The first missionary journey of Paul, also known as Saul of Tarsus, had its roots in the church of Antioch. Members of the church perceived from the Holy Spirit that they were to send Barnabas and Paul on a missionary journey. Barnabas and Paul, bringing Barnabas' cousin John Mark along, went down to Seleucia from Antioch and sailed from there to Cyprus. These men proclaimed the gospel boldly all across Cyprus and at times met with opposition. From Paphos, Paul and his companions sailed to Perga in Pamphylia, where John Mark left them to return to Jerusalem. Paul and Barnabas continued to proclaim the gospel throughout such places as Pisidian Antioch, Iconium, Lystra, Derbe, and Attalia. From Attalia they sailed back to Antioch.

Some time later Paul said to Barnabas, "Let us return and visit the brethren in every city in which we proclaimed the word of the Lord and see how they are." (Acts 15:36). Barnabas wanted to take John Mark with them, but Paul did not think it wise to take him, because he had deserted them in Pamphylia and had not continued with them in their work. Paul and Barnabas had such a sharp disagreement over this that they parted company. Barnabas took John Mark and sailed for Cyprus, but Paul chose Silas, and proceeded through Syria and Cilicia. Paul perceived John Mark as letting them down and that John Mark could not be counted upon in another missionary journey. Details of why John Mark departed Paul and Barnabas earlier are not fully known. Perhaps it can be attributed to youth, immaturity, lack of dedication, hard conditions over an arduous journey, opposition or a combination of these factors. Regardless, there are clear indications of change in both Paul and John Mark later in their lives. John Mark would continue developing in the Lord and later write the second book of the New Testament, the Gospel of Mark. Paul would later acknowledge the spiritual development in John Mark and consider him a dear friend.

People make mistakes, but people can change. It may require more dedication, discipline, or giving up friendships with people who create bad influences. The giving and proper reception of wise counsel can be impactive in the redirection of lives. Let us remember that diamonds in the rough are so often made into beautiful, shining gems. Through proper leadership and discipleship, an individual can often be redirected and influenced to achieve his full potential. "For I am confident of this very thing, that He who began a good work in you will perfect it until the day of Christ Jesus." (Philippians 1:6). The Bible makes it clear that God wants us all to move forward in Him and will assist us in our efforts to do so. We need to be conscious of this in our lives and as we help others.

8
Pride Is A Thief

Naaman was Captain of the army of the King of Aram and well respected as a valiant leader. Unfortunately, he had developed leprosy. In his house was a young Israelite girl who revealed to him that there was a mighty prophet in Samaria who could bring Naaman healing. The King of Aram sent Naaman on his way to find Elisha, the prophet. Naaman, through the King of Israel, came to Elisha's doorway with his horses and chariots and gifts. He had found the prophet's house.

Elisha sent a messenger to Naaman to tell him to wash in the Jordan River seven times and that he would be healed. Naaman was furious. Here he was the Captain of the army of the King of Aram and the prophet did not even come out to see him. These words of washing in the Jordan River seemed trivial to Naaman's ears as his pride was strongly kindled within him. Fortunately, Naaman had wise servants that pressed upon him to do what the prophet had told him to do through the messenger. Naaman gave in and went to the Jordan River and dipped seven times. His flesh was restored as a little child. Naaman was so glad that he had put away his pride and did as he was told. He returned to offer Elisha a gift for his healing but Elisha did not take one. Elisha knew it was God who had healed Naaman and not himself.

Pride robs many of blessings. Naaman almost let pride rob him of his healing. Such a difference can be seen in one who has a spirit of humility versus one who has a spirit of pride. Pride has ruined relationships and prevented people from receiving from God throughout time. A wheat field at harvest time provides an interesting example for study. Some wheat heads will be seen standing much more straight and erect than others. One may perceive at first glance that these erect ones are filled with grain, but in reality, the ones with the bowed heads are the ones filled with full, golden kernels of wheat. Shun pride and be of humble spirit towards others and the promises of God. "A man's pride will bring him low, But a humble spirit will obtain honor." (Proverbs 29:23). Don't let pride rob you of blessings.

9

An Act Of Love

Passover and the Feast of Unleavened Bread were soon approaching with the chief priests and teachers of the law looking for some sly way to arrest and kill Jesus. Thus, one sees the continuing mind set of these leaders as they plot against the Lord. The arrest and crucifixion draws nearer.

Jesus was in the home of Simon the Leper in Bethany when a woman came in with an alabaster jar of very expensive perfume, made of pure nard. She proceeded to break the jar and pour it on his head. This caused indignation among the others present. Why waste such expensive perfume when it could be sold and the money given to the poor. Jesus said, "Let her alone; why do you bother her? She has done a good deed to Me. For the poor you will always have with you, and whenever you wish, you can do them good; but you do not always have Me. She had done what she could; she has anointed my body beforehand for the burial. And truly I say to you, wherever the gospel is preached in the whole world, that also which this woman has done shall be spoken of in memory of her." (Mark 14:6–9). Jesus foresaw his arrest and crucifixion were near.

One may say this woman and her actions were insignificant. Jesus didn't see it that way. She gave a costly gift out of great love and Jesus ensured it was recorded in the Bible for multitudes to read. Giving in love towards others is to be commended. One needs to take note of this and extend love towards others. Love is an action word in the Bible that has significant impact on lives in a cruel and harsh world when applied. Building friendships and relationships through love is more important than the accumulation of material goods. Material goods will pass away but friendships and relationships will carry into eternity. "Beloved, let us love one another, for love is from God; and every one who loves is born of God and knows God. The one who does not love does not know God, for God is love." (I John 4:7–8).

10
Courage Of Conviction

The courage of conviction can clearly be seen in the life of Caleb. Caleb, the son of Jephunneh, was one of the twelve spies sent by Moses to scout out the promised land of Canaan. One may recall Caleb and Joshua were the only two who did not allow the difficulties to minimize God, and as such, presented an unpopular minority report urging the tribes to move out at once to take the land.

Moses, while at Kadesh-Barnea, sent out twelve spies to spy out the land of Canaan. This was after the exodus from Egypt and crossing of the Red Sea. The spies returned from Canaan after forty days with clusters of fruit from the land and reconnaissance reports of Canaan's inhabitants and fortifications. Ten of the spies acknowledged it was a prosperous land but said it was filled with fortified cities and strong people. They felt as grasshoppers in their own sight and did not believe they could take the land. Caleb and Joshua, on the other hand, said the Israelites should go forth and take the land for they were well able. The majority sided with the report of the ten spies, believing the Israelites were not able to take the land. Caleb and Joshua stood as a minority but refused to change their convictions of belief. They believed God was with them and that they were well able to possess the land.

The story from this point is well known in the history of Israel. The Lord directed Moses to lead the Israelites through the wilderness for forty years. Those that had doubted God perished in the wilderness; however, Caleb and Joshua, were allowed to enter the promised land. They were the only two members of their generation allowed to do so.

Adverse circumstances were again to face Caleb. The Israelites were now in the promised land. Caleb, desirous of the area surrounding Hebron, had to conquer the well fortified cities of the Anakim. Caleb was 85 years old and the circumstances were not favorable. This did not deter Caleb. He was a man of conviction and believed within himself that he would gain the victory. Victory came.

Many people over time have given way to the majority when they know they're right and the majority is wrong. Many people lose their confidence and convictions when they see the circumstances that arise against them. Then there are people who will stand firm in their convictions, no matter what. They refuse to accept defeat and waver not. I'm reminded of a young boy who was seen by a passerby petting an old dog. The man asked, "Can your dog run fast?" The boy replied, "No, not very, but he can stand fast." Standing on our convictions, when we know we're right, will ultimately bear fruit in our lives. Waver not and remain steadfast. Victory comes.

11

A Servant's Heart

In the days when the judges ruled, there was a famine in the land, and a man from Bethlehem in Judah, together with his wife and two sons, went to live for awhile in Moab. The man's name was Elimelech, his wife's name Naomi, and the names of his two sons were Mahlon and Kilion.

Elimelech died and Naomi was left with her two sons who married Moabite women, one named Orpah and the other Ruth. After they had lived there about 10 years, both Mahlon and Kilion died, and Naomi was then left without her two sons.

Naomi set out to Judah, accompanied by her two daughters-in-law, when she heard famine was now past. En route she urged each of her daughters-in-law to return to their mother's home. They all wept, but Ruth absolutely refused to depart Naomi's side. Thus, Naomi returned from Moab accompanied by Ruth the Moabitess, arriving in Bethlehem as the barley harvest was beginning.

Ruth proceeded to glean in the fields behind the harvesters. As it turned out, she found herself working in a field belonging to Boaz, who was from the clan of Elimelech. Boaz took notice of Ruth and acknowledged all she had done for her mother-in-law. Ruth gleaned in the field until evening and then threshed the barley she had gathered. Ultimately, Ruth, a woman of noble character, married Boaz.

Ruth was a kind and humble individual. She continued to show kindness and care towards her mother-in-law when she had been released from any commitment. Self-denial and self-sacrifice can clearly be seen in the life of Ruth. As she remained faithful to her mother-in-law, God remained faithful to her. Ruth received favor in Judah and became part of David's genealogy.

I visited the Dead Sea in Israel during an assignment in the Middle East. They call it dead because it receives water from the Jordan River but gives none of it out to the surrounding area. Its water is exceptionally salty, bitter in taste, oily to feel and leaves a yellowish stain. No fish live in its water and its shores bear collections of salt. At 1292 feet below sea level, it is an exceedingly hot and arid region. The Dead Sea portrays just the opposite of a servant's heart in geographical form, that of a selfish and self-centered picture. A servant's heart, on the other hand, paints a much more beautiful, lush and fruitful scene. "Do nothing from selfishness or empty conceit, but with humility of mind let each of you regard one another as more important than himself; do not merely look out for your own personal interests, but also for the interests of others." (Philippians 2:3–4).

12
You're Not Alone

The king of Aram was at war with Israel. He would make plans and consistently be thwarted by the king of Israel. Enraged over these events, he called his servants together to determine the problem. One of the king's servants revealed that Elisha, the prophet, was revealing the king's secrets to the king of Israel.

After finding out that Elisha was in Dothan, the King of Aram sent a great army with horses and chariots to surround the city at night. Elisha's servant, rising early, beheld the great army and approached Elisha in fear. Elisha told his servant not to fear and that more were with them than with the opposing army. Elisha then prayed that his servant's eyes would be opened. The Lord opened the servant's eyes so he could see into the spiritual realm. Elisha's servant beheld that the mountain was full of horses and chariots of fire all around them. Elisha then prayed that the opposing army be struck with blindness and so it was.

The servant of Elisha saw great problems for them through his physical eyes. His eyes certainly were not on God in this situation. One gets into trouble when one looks at problems strictly with the five physical senses. One prays and then frets as the mountain seems even greater than before. Elisha had his eyes on God, prayed and got results. Our eyes need to be opened to the inheritance we have in God's promises. As Elisha, let us keep our eyes on God and trust in his deliverance. Let us not focus and dwell on the problems, but let us focus on God's promises and His favor. Find scriptures to stand on, pray, and cast your care on Him thanking Him for meeting the need. God is faithful.

Notice in this passage that there was a multitude of angels around Elisha and his servant. God has mighty angels that serve God's people and assist in answered prayer. "Are they not all ministering spirits, sent out to render service for the sake of those who will inherit salvation?" (Hebrews 1:14). You have good company and you're not alone.

13
Deception And Lies

This story begins with Ananias and his wife Sapphira. They had sold a piece of property and pretended to give all the money to the apostles while keeping part of it for themselves. This was at a time in the early church when believers were sharing their possessions. Peter responded to Ananias, "Ananias, why has Satan filled your heart to lie to the Holy Spirit, and to keep back some of the price of the land? While it remained unsold, did it not remain your own? And after it was sold, was it not under your control? Why is it that you have conceived this deed in your heart? You have not lied to men, but to God." (Acts 5:3–4). Ananias fell dead after hearing these words. Three hours later Sapphira appeared before Peter and met a similar fate because of her deceit.

One might believe this a hard story upon a quick glance since Ananias and Sapphira gave some of their money to the church. However, money isn't the key issue in this story; although, giving is clearly encouraged in the Bible. The Christians were free to give their possessions if they chose to do so and they were also free not to give their possessions. This was a matter of choice. The key issue is that Ananias and Sapphira devised a plan of deception. It was conceived in their hearts and acted upon.

Honesty should be practiced as a way of living. Deception and lies work ill will towards others for the better of one's own personal ambitions and desires. Ultimately, deceptions and lies will work against one and harden one's heart when it appears one has gained. One will reap what one sows. Ananias and Sapphira happened to reap quickly in their situation. A package of deception and lies with a nice bow and wrapping may appear to generate favorable results but it's empty. Honesty speaks much better of a person. "Do not lie to one another, since you laid aside the old self with its evil practices, and have put on the new self who is being renewed to a true knowledge according to the image of the One who created him." (Colossians 3:9–10).

14
Principles Are Important

Isaac's wife Rebekah gave birth to Esau and Jacob, fraternal twins, when Isaac was 60 years old. Esau was born first with Jacob following holding onto Esau's heel. When the boys grew up, Esau became a skilled hunter, a man of the field, but Jacob was a peaceful man living in tents.

One day Esau came in from the field and was famished. He approached Jacob, who had cooked some stew, to give him some. Jacob said he would if Esau would sell him his birthright. Esau then agreed and sold Jacob his birthright. Jacob proceeded to give Esau bread and lentil stew; and Esau ate and drank and went on his way.

The birthright of the eldest son gave him precedence over his brothers and assured him a double share of his father's inheritance. It could be forfeited by committing a serious sin or it could be bartered, as in this instance. The agreement between Esau and Jacob was solemnized by an oath. [1] Thus, Esau despised his birthright.

One might be quick to criticize Esau for this shallow and shortsighted decision. Truly, it was just that, but what happens when one compromises one's principles and gives in to peer pressure influence or lustful desires. Is this not shallow and shortsighted? How often does one wish one had not compromised one's principles after it's done? Maintaining one's principles will help build one's character. Equally, the reciprocal is true; it tears it down. "A good name is to be more desired than great riches, Favor is better than silver and gold." (Proverbs 22:1). Excellent character and the reputation that goes with it are to be highly valued.

15

A Fervent Prayer

Elkanah had two wives who were named Hannah and Peninnah. Peninnah had children but Hannah had none. Polygamy was allowed in the case of a childless first marriage and of a levirate marriage but it often caused much misery and was not in accordance with God's ideal for marriage.[2] Peninnah often would provoke Hannah and consistently hurt her feelings since she was childless. Hannah shed many tears over her predicament.

Hannah, however, petitioned the Lord over her situation. She cried to God from the depths of her heart for a son and vowed she would dedicate him to lifelong levitical service if God would grant this petition. Her prayer was fervent and spoken with great desire. Hannah's prayer touched the compassion of the Lord and He enabled her to give birth to a son. Hannah named her son Samuel and dedicated him to the Lord. Oh! how Hannah praised and exalted God in thanksgiving for her blessing. Samuel was to grow up and become a mighty prophet in Israel.

Two things come out immediately when one looks at Hannah's prayer. First, it was fervent. Secondly, she sincerely desired her petition. God has not changed and still has great compassion. A fervent prayer from the heart of a believer will avail much and touch the compassion of our Lord. (James 5:16). God wants to bless his children. Pray from your heart and expect.

16
Be As Abel

Abel became a keeper of sheep and Cain a tiller of the ground. Thus, Abel brought the firstlings of his flock and of their fat portions as his offering while Cain brought some fruit of the ground for his. The Lord had regard for Abel's offering but He had no regard for Cain's offering. This made Cain very angry. He later murdered Abel as a result of it.

This story deserves further analysis. Initially, one asks the question why was Abel's offering acceptable and Cain's not? I believe it was a case of attitude. Abel appeared to approach his offering with reverence toward God by offering his very best. Cain, on the other hand, brought perhaps whatever fruit he picked up. God looks on the heart and I believe He saw in Abel a penitent attitude while in Cain He saw a more proud one. Abel sought God's eyes while Cain performed his obligation. This perception becomes more reinforced when Cain reveals his true nature by getting angry at Abel and murdering him. Abel did no harm to Cain. One with a penitent heart would recognize his hypocrisy towards God and ask for forgiveness. One with a corrupt heart diverts attention and responsibility away from self and places it on others for one's problems. God would have restored fellowship with Cain if Cain would have been receptive to it. God is a righteous God.

Attitude is important to God. One needs to recognize this when one gives tithes, offerings, time and service towards the furtherance of His kingdom. One needs to give of sustenance and service with joy for it is an honor to serve Him. Don't ever approach God with an attitude of obligation, but always approach Him with reverence, willingness and humility. Be as Abel in your attitude and get God's attention in your life. It makes a difference in you and to God.

17

One Can Run But One Cannot Hide

Jonah received word from the Lord to go and preach in Nineveh. Jonah, not desiring to do this, ran from the Lord and boarded a ship for Tarshish. Jonah's troubles were about to begin. A violent storm arose and Jonah, troubled, confessed to the crew that he was the cause of it since he was running from the Lord. Thus, the crew threw Jonah overboard and the sea became calm.

Jonah was swallowed by a great fish and remained inside of it for three days and three nights. It was during this time that Jonah prayed to the Lord and repented of his rebellion. At the end of the three days and three nights the fish vomited Jonah onto dry land. This time Jonah obeyed the Lord and went to Nineveh. Jonah boldly proclaimed once he arrived there that the great city of Nineveh was to be destroyed. The Ninevites believed God and declared a fast, and all of them, from the greatest to the least, put on sackcloth. The king of Nineveh, himself, took off his royal robes and covered himself with sackcloth. When God saw what they did and how they turned from their evil ways, He had compassion and did not bring destruction.

Jonah, knowing what was right to do, refused and rebelled. He suffered grave consequences in the sea as a result of that rebellion. Rebellion to what is right will reap unfavorable results. One may think one can run from the truth or the problem but it will catch up with one sooner or later. The inner voice of Jonah's spirit would not let him hide. So it is with mankind. The inner voice of one's spirit is there for a reason. "The spirit of man is the lamp of the Lord, Searching all the innermost parts of his being." (Proverbs 20:27). The phrase "Let your conscience be your guide" has merit.

18

A Righteous Man

Weakness was great on the earth as the Lord grieved over His creation. Corruption was rampant and violence filled the earth. Noah, however, was a righteous man who found favor in the eyes of God. He maintained continual fellowship with the Lord and walked uprightly. As such, God was to spare Noah and his family during the great flood that was coming.

God directed Noah to make an ark and gave him specific dimensions for building it. He warned him of the forthcoming flood and Noah proceeded to spend close to 120 years building the ark. Talk about a man of faith. Noah did as the Lord commanded and then gathered his household and all kinds of animals and fowl onto it. Then the rain fell on the earth for forty days and forty nights. The water increased greatly on the earth and the ark began to float on the surface of it. Mankind and the rest of the animals and fowl outside the ark perished. The water surrounding the ark steadily receded after the great rain with the ark settling on the mountains of Ararat after about 150 days.

So many things can be gained from looking at the life of Noah but I'll just focus on his righteous living. The earth was filled with corruption and violence yet he walked uprightly and in fellowship with God. Today, one can turn on the television news broadcast and see comparable corruption, evil and violence virtually on any continent in the world. It wasn't pleasing for God to see great evil then and it's not pleasing now. Noah was spared, the ungodly were not. "AND IF IT IS WITH DIFFICULTY THE RIGHTEOUS IS SAVED, WHAT WILL BECOME OF THE GODLESS MAN AND THE SINNER?" (I Peter 5:18).

Walk in fellowship with God and receive his favor and blessings. "For it is Thou who dost bless the righteous man, O Lord, Thou dost surround him with favor as with a shield." (Psalm 5:12). "The eyes of the Lord are toward the righteous, And His ears are open to their cry." (Psalm 34:15). "The Lord is far from the wicked, But He hears the prayer of the righteous." (Proverbs 15:29). Choose to be a righteous man in the Lord. It pays dividends.

19
Parental Discipline Is Important

Hophni and Phinehas, the sons of Eli the high priest, were guilty of taking more of the sacrifice than their allotted portion and generally despising the offerings of the Lord. His sons were even guilty of laying with women who served at the entrance of the tent of meeting. Eli did not have his personal house in order which led to the prophet's prediction of destruction for the priestly family of Eli.

Eli's two sons were to later perish in a battle between the Israelites and Philistines. Thirty thousand Israelites fell in this battle in which the Philistines captured the ark of God. Eli, 98 years old, hearing of the deaths of Hophni and Phinehas and the capture of the ark of God, fell off his seat backwards and died from breaking his neck. The later massacre of the priests of Nob and the transfer of the priesthood to the family of Zadok in the time of Solomon were in line with the prophet's original prediction.

One can learn from looking at Eli's family situation. It was a case of rebellious children and failure in the area of parental discipline. The Bible provides definitive guidance for parents in the area of discipline. "He who spares his rod hates his son, But he who loves him disciplines him diligently." (Proverbs 13:24). Basically, as nice as I can say this, one does not love one's child if proper discipline is not administered. "Train up a child in the way he should go, Even when he is old he will not depart from it." (Proverbs 22:6). Teaching a child what is right and wrong is the responsibility of parents. Prisons are full of men and women who never received parental discipline and godly instruction as children. Parents have keen responsibilities in this area and failure to execute those responsibilities will be revealed in the lives of their children as they grow up. Discipline in love and your children will be the better for it.

20

Unity In Heart

Nebuchadnezzar had conquered Jerusalem and led many Israelites into captivity during the 586 B.C. time frame.[3] Solomon's temple had been destroyed and much of Israel devastated. Even so, in time, the walls of Jerusalem would be rebuilt.

Nehemiah, cupbearer to King Artaxerxes, was to be instrumental in the rebuilding of Jerusalem's walls. King Artaxerxes noticed Nehemiah had a saddened heart and inquired into reasons why. Nehemiah, still in exile with other Israelites, wanted to return to Jerusalem and rebuild the city. The king granted Nehemiah's wish. Nehemiah, with others, returned to Jerusalem and set their minds and efforts towards rebuilding Jerusalem's walls and gates. The time frame was around 444 B.C.[4] Great effort and teamwork were clearly required. The people worked with all their heart. Throughout their arduous efforts they were faced with opposition. Sanballat, Geshem and others in the area plotted against Nehemiah's efforts. Much of the time many of the Israelites stood guard with spears, shields and bows while others diligently worked. Eventually, after 52 days, the wall around Jerusalem was completed. Nehemiah's enemies, upon completion of the wall, lost their self-confidence because they realized that this great task had been done with the help of the Lord. Exiles were now free to return.

This important event in the history of Israel was accomplished through the teamwork and unity of the people involved. Division will work against an organization or unit but unity magnifies its force. A leader must determine his goals and objectives, and through leadership, get them into the heart of his people. Unity in heart produces great success.

21
Courage To Confront

Ahab, at Elijah's request, sent a message throughout Israel to gather the prophets of Baal and the Asherah at Mt. Carmel. Baal was the rain and fertility god of the Canaanites and the Asherah was the chief goddess of Tyre and mother of Baal. Much of Israel had forsaken the commandments of the Lord and pursued paganism. The worship of these false deities included animal sacrifices, male and female prostitution, and even human sacrifices. [5] So it was that 450 prophets of Baal gathered with Elijah and many other Israelites on Mt. Carmel, located near current day Haifa.

Elijah, a mighty prophet of God, challenged the prophets of Baal to determine the true God. His challenge was that they each cut up an ox and place it on wood without starting a fire. Then the God who answered by fire on the sacrifice would be known as the true God. The prophets of Baal went first and cried out to Baal to answer by fire. They leaped around the altar and loudly petitioned Baal with no answer. Elijah mocked them for he knew Baal was a false god. They continued to rave throughout the whole day with no results.

It was now Elijah's turn. He arranged his altar and cut the ox into pieces and laid it on the wood. He ordered that water be placed abundantly on the ox and the wood underneath it. Then Elijah began to petition the God of Abraham, Isaac and Jacob. The Lord immediately sent fire that consumed the ox, wood and water all around the sacrifice. The onlooking people were awed and recognized the true God of Israel that day. Then Elijah told the people to seize the prophets of Baal and bring them to the Kishon brook where Elijah slew them.

Elijah towers as a mighty man of God in this scene. Confident and trusting in God, he confronts the rampant evil of the land head-on and experiences great victory. Many were calling evil as good and good as evil. Today it's the same in many ways throughout the world. Men are still calling evil as good and good as evil. Let us, as Elijah, be confident in God and stand up in our land for what is good. "Righteousness exalts a nation, But sin is a disgrace to any people." (Proverbs 14:34). "You are the light of the world, A city on a hill cannot be hidden." (Matthew 5:14). Christian principles and ideals are important to the success of individual lives and to the society as a whole. Let your light shine and be strong in the Lord for light dispels darkness. Your light is important and it does make a difference.

22

Sin In The Camp

The Israelites had just experienced a great victory at Jericho after crossing the Jordan River into Canaan. They had cooperated with God and received victory after shouting at the precise time of their seventh day march in accordance with God's instructions. The city was under the ban which meant Jericho was to be completely devoted to God as the first fruits of Canaan. No booty was to be taken by anyone. Achan, however, broke faith with this direction and secretly hid booty.

The Israelites, confident after their great victory, decided to attack Ai. Joshua sent men to spy out the area, and based on their report, sent only about 3,000 men to attack the city. Unfortunately, for the Israelites, the city of Ai repelled the attack and pushed them into retreat with 36 Israelites being slain. This greatly disturbed the rest of the Israelites as Joshua cried out to God in distress.

God revealed to Joshua that things were previously taken in Jericho that were under the ban. Joshua took immediate action to determine who violated this ban. Ultimately, the violation was traced to Achan who had taken a beautiful mantle from Shinar, 200 sheckels of silver and a bar of gold 50 sheckels in weight. The booty was found concealed in the earth inside Achan's tent after Achan confessed his sin. Achan, his family and animals were then stoned and burned in the valley of Achor. This sin was dealt with swiftly and quickly purged.

There was sin in Joshua's camp. He had lost God's protection in the battle of Ai and he had to deal with this sin. Pastors and congregations need to be sensitive to Achan's activity. Today, many churches have faltered through division, gossip, rebellion, strife or other sins. An open Heaven over a church is a true blessing but it can be hindered or even closed if sin develops unbridled in a congregation. Unbridled sin must be confronted and dealt with. Joshua confronted the sin in his camp and gained victory the next time the Israelites attacked Ai.

From personal experience I've seen how one or two people with bad and negative attitudes can affect others in small units or organizations. There's a phrase, "A rotten apple spoils the bushel". I've seen units turned around for the better when these problems were addressed and I've seen the consequences when the problems were not addressed. A seedling with small roots can easily be pulled from the ground but as time passes it grows in size and strength and the roots go deeper.

23

Jealousy Is Not Worth It

Shortly after the destruction of the pursuing Egyptians in the Red Sea, the Israelites began to celebrate in song and dance. Miriam, sister of Moses and Aaron, took a timbrel in her hand and led the other women who had timbrels in dance. There was great celebration unto the Lord for he had delivered the Israelites from Pharaoh's army.

Miriam, a prophetess, appears to have had a foremost place in the women's sacred songs and dances. She had been more than just a sister to Moses. She had been a caring and close companion to him for 40 years now. Her situation was to quickly change, however, because of jealously. Jealousy kindles misguided pride as it did when Miriam and Aaron spoke against Moses because of his marriage to a Cushite (Ethiopian) woman. Murmuring began and the Lord heard it. Then suddenly the Lord called Moses, Aaron and Miriam to the tent of meeting. The Lord came down in a pillar of cloud and stood at the doorway of the tent and spoke to Aaron and Miriam. The Lord let it be known that He was not happy with their murmuring against His humble servant Moses. The cloud departed, and behold, Miriam was leprous. Moses immediately cried out to the Lord for her healing. The Lord said after she had been cast outside the camp for seven days to bear her shame then she could be received again. The open matter of her sin called for open punishment. After the seven days, Miriam was restored to the camp and the Israelites moved from Hazeroth to the wilderness of Paran.

Jealousy destroys lives. It works at the inside of a person causing them to act cruelly and improperly. It eats at one like a cancerous sin. It's not worth the consequences and should be avoided with an attitude of humility. It worked against Miriam and it will work against you. "For where jealousy and selfish ambition exist, there is disorder and every evil thing." (James 3:16). Avoid jealousy and walk humbly before the Lord, casting your cares on Him. You'll be glad you did.

24
Commitment Counts

Commitment to duty, vocation or goals is so important to success. The fruits of commitment in one's life can even be seen many years after one's death. The commitment of Paul, the most prominent figure in the Book of Acts, bears convincing proof of this statement.

Paul, after his conversion to Christianity, was to conduct three significant missionary journeys in his life. The first was conducted across Cyprus with Barnabas. The second was conducted with Silas and was to lay the foundation for the founding and development of a new nation, the United States of America. One might be puzzled about this statement but greater analysis will reveal its validity. Paul and Silas were traveling through Asia, current day Turkey, at the time. Paul, while in Troas, received a vision from God of a man from Macedonia. This man was appealing for Paul and Silas to come to Macedonia and help them. Macedonia was an ancient kingdom across the Aegean Sea and north of Greece. Paul and Silas immediately sought to go to Macedonia. They set out to sea from Troas and eventually came to Philippi, a leading city of Macedonia.

Paul and Silas evangelized in this area and were thrown into prison as a result of their efforts. It appeared bleak for both of them; however, while praying and praising God at midnight a remarkable event occurred. An earthquake came and their shackles were unfastened and the prison doors opened. The jailer, roused from his sleep, drew his sword and was about to kill himself thinking the prisoners had escaped. Paul and Silas yelled not to harm himself for they were there. Consequently, Paul and Silas led this Philippian jailer and his family into salvation. This was significant for it provided the impetus for the evangelization of Europe. It was from Macedonia that the gospel and Christianity spread to Europe and ultimately to America.

Christopher Columbus discovered the new world in 1492. Columbus, of Christian roots, felt God's hand on this endeavor and believed God watched over him and his voyage en route to this discovery. Many people would later flee Europe in pursuit of their Christian beliefs and help colonize much of America. The Pilgrims, Puritans and others were to come and help lay the foundation for this forthcoming nation. Columbus, Pilgrims, Puritans and others can clearly trace their beliefs back to the missionary efforts of Paul.

Paul unequivocally was a committed man. He was whipped, beaten, stoned and shipwrecked during his missionary journeys. Yet, he did not quit; nothing could deter him in his efforts. As a result of his commitment, years after his death, America was conceived as a Christian nation. Commitment to our endeavors and Christian walks will also affect the lives of others and the kingdom of God. Commitment counts.

25
Never Give Up

People in all walks of life have dreams. Most people want to succeed and are delighted when their dreams come true. Hard work is important but there is another aspect that is often overlooked. That aspect is inner endurance or patience. This clearly can be seen in the life of Joseph, one of Jacob's twelve sons. I will summarize his life in the following paragraphs and then highlight some important points in conclusion.

Joseph received two dreams from God that revealed to him he was to be elevated in life. Joseph revealed these dreams to his brothers, but they became jealous of him. This jealousy stirred within them and led them to sell their brother into slavery to a caravan of Ishmaelites. The saga of Joseph was about to begin.

The Ishmaelites, once in Egypt, turned and sold Joseph to Potiphar, one of Pharaoh's officials, the Captain of the Guard. The Lord was with Joseph and gave him success in everything he did. As such, Potiphar put him in charge of his household and entrusted everything he owned to Joseph's care. Potiphar's house prospered, but Joseph who was well-built and handsome, was noticed by Potiphar's wife. She attempted to seduce him but Joseph fled from her sight and refused to violate the trust Potiphar had placed in him. Potiphar, believing his wife's lie that Joseph had tried to seduce her, sent Joseph to prison.

Joseph, now in prison, met with the cupbearer and baker the king had sent to prison. They both revealed dreams they had had to Joseph. Joseph, with God's help, successfully interpreted their dreams. The cupbearer, who was supposed to help Joseph when he was released from prison, forgot about Joseph. Joseph, with another chance to give up all hope, cast not away his confidence.

Two full years had passed and Pharaoh then had a dream. Pharaoh sent for his magicians and wise men, but they could not interpret his dream. The cupbearer suddenly remembered Joseph and told Pharaoh about him. Pharaoh immediately sent for Joseph from the dungeon. Joseph, again with God's help, successfully interpreted Pharaoh's dream. As a result, Joseph was appointed in charge of Pharaoh's palace and affairs. Joseph was elevated and ran the whole land of Egypt, second only to Pharaoh.

Joseph, a man who trusted in God, refused to walk by sight. Something in him told him victory was coming. Joseph was sold into slavery; falsely accused; and placed in prison. Joseph could have easily given up all hope and accepted defeat. Yet, Joseph, worked hard wherever he was placed and retained a firm conviction within himself victory was coming. Adverse situations came but Joseph guarded his heart, endured and triumphed. His trust in God and inner endurance led him to victory. He never gave up. We can gain as we analyze this story and apply it to our lives. Never give up. "And Jesus said to him, 'If you can! All things are possible to him who believes.' " (Mark 9:23).

26
Resist Pressure To Compromise

Daniel excelled in his assignment as an administrator in the kingdom. King Darius noticed his performance and planned to set him over all his affairs. This greatly upset the other administrators as they attempted to find charges in some area they could bring against Daniel. Unfortunately for them, they could find no corruption for Daniel was trustworthy, honest and scrupulous in all his governmental affairs. These administrators, realizing Daniel to be a man of integrity, then plotted to have the king issue a decree that anyone who prayed to any god or man during the next 30 days, except to King Darius, would be thrown into the lions' den. Realizing Daniel was a man of prayer, they spied upon Daniel and found him praying and asking God for help.

The decree, in accordance with the laws of the Medes and Persians, could not be annulled. The devious administrators knew this and quickly reported to King Darius on Daniel's actions. King Darius, holding Daniel in high esteem, was greatly distressed, but nevertheless, ordered Daniel into the lions' den since he could not alter his decree. The den was sealed and the king spent the night worrying about Daniel. At first light, the king approached the den and found Daniel completely safe and untouched. Daniel immediately acknowledged God's angelic protection over him. This led King Darius to proclaim the God of Daniel as the true and living God throughout his land.

Daniel refused to compromise on his relationship to God. He trusted in God and prayed to him daily. His walk with God was of utmost importance in his life. He would not compromise his relationship in spite of the pressure to do so. The devil consistently brings pressure against Christians to compromise their Christian principles and walks with God. He'll use all sorts of devious plots and tricks to cause Christians to compromise. Daniel refused to compromise; gained the victory; gave credit to God; and saw God honored in the land of the Medes and Persians. People are watching Christians as they watched Daniel. Do not compromise under pressure. Look to God, trust in Him and gain the victory. "Create in me a clean heart, O God, And renew a steadfast spirit within me." (Psalm 51:10).

27

Sin Has Its Rewards

David arose from bed one evening and walked on the roof of his house. He saw a beautiful woman bathing from his view. Inquiring about the woman, he found her to be Bathsheba, wife of Uriah the Hittite. Homes in this region often had enclosed courtyards that were considered part of the houses. A woman, bathing herself by lamplight, would not necessarily be considered immodest for she would be in her house. Further, David's house was situated on the higher elevation of Mt. Zion, giving him a commanding view from his house.[6]

David sent for Bathsheba and yielded to his temptation of lust by laying with Bathsheba who became pregnant. David, in an attempt to cover his sin, sent for Uriah who had been away in battle with Joab and the rest of the army. He told Uriah to spend some time at his home, but Uriah, dedicated to his men and mission, refused to indulge in this special pleasure while the rest of the troops were away in battle. As such, David sent Uriah back to Joab with a special letter that told Joab to place Uriah in the front line of the fiercest battle with special instructions to ensure Uriah's death. Joab carried out David's directions and Uriah perished in battle just as David planned.

David brought Bathsheba into his house and married her after she completed the time of mourning for Uriah. Sin may be concealed from many, but our omniscient God sees it. David was guilty of adultery and murder and God dealt with him. God sent Nathan, the prophet, to confront David with his deeds. God told David through Nathan that judgment was coming to his household.

Sin has its rewards and they're not worth it. David's household was never the same after his sins. God forgave him after he sought forgiveness, but his household was to experience the fulfillment of Nathan's prophecies. (II Samuel 12:10–11, 14). The child born to David and Bathsheba from their sinful union died on the seventh day after his birth. (II Samuel 12:18). The prophecies were further fulfilled in the violent deaths of his sons Amnon (II Samuel 13:28–29) and Absalom (II Samuel 18:15); the rape of his daughter Tamar (II Samuel 13:14); and Absalom's public appropriation of David's royal concubines. (II Samuel 16:22). David's sins were not worth it.

Many marriages have been ruined through flings of lust. Many lives have been ruined through riotous living. Commitment of crimes generated from greed, hatred and rebellion has destroyed lives. The fruits of sin may appear good for the moment, but upon closer examination you'll see they're rotten. A man reaps what he sows.

God provided us a plan of salvation and guidelines for living a prosperous and fruitful live. Adhering to the Lord's plan and guidance for our lives will produce the rewards worth having.

28

Faith Pays Off

Jesus had recently returned to Capernaum. His reputation of teaching and power over demons and sickness was quickly spreading. Many upon finding out that He was in Capernaum flocked to the home where He was staying. So many came that there was no longer any room in the home or even near the door as Jesus taught them.

Then four men approached the home with a paralytic. They were unable to get through the doorway to Jesus for the crowd was so great. They could have returned home figuring it was not God's will for them to receive from Jesus. They could have done this but they didn't. Instead they proceeded to dig an opening in the roof and let down the pallet on which the paralytic was lying through it. Jesus, seeing their faith, forgave the man's sins and healed him. He dealt with the man's spiritual need and then his physical one.

Jesus is no different today. He is the same yesterday and today, yes and forever. (Hebrews 13:8). The paralytic received his healing as Jesus saw the faith of that group. Repeatedly, throughout the New Testament, we see Jesus filled with compassion and healing those that came to Him in faith. The four men who carried the paralytic could have turned away saying the circumstances won't allow them to receive from Jesus. However, they would not be denied. They would not allow the circumstances to prevent them from receiving from the Lord.

Let us also not allow temporal circumstances, no matter what they are, prevent us from receiving from God. Let us focus on the promises of God and get them into our hearts. The storms of life or adversities say one thing but the Word of God says victory. The blood of Jesus provides for us salvation and whatever we need to live good and prosperous lives. Let us remain steadfast after we pray and receive from the Lord for He wants to truly bless us. "And without faith it is impossible to please Him, for he who comes to God must believe that He is, and that He is a rewarder of those that seek Him." (Hebrews 11:6). "And Jesus answered saying to them, Have faith in God. Truly I say to you, whoever says to this mountain, Be taken up and cast into the sea, and does not doubt in his heart, but believes that what he says is going to happen, it shall be granted him. Therefore I say to you, all things for which you pray and ask, believe that you have received them, and they shall be granted you." (Mark 11:22–24). Let our words and corresponding actions confirm what we're standing for. Be a doer of the Word and receive your reward.

29

Obedience Nets Results

Jesus was standing by the Sea of Galilee and teaching the multitude that were pressing around Him. Spotting two boats by the water's edge, He got into one of them which happened to belong to Peter. Jesus asked Peter to push out a little from the land as He continued to teach the people. After He had finished teaching, He asked Peter to go into deeper water and let down his nets for some fish.

Peter was a fisherman by trade. He had worked all night and caught nothing. He had already taken his nets out of the boat to wash them and was probably tired and ready to go home and get some rest. Here Jesus was telling him to go fishing again. Peter's reaction to Jesus was not one of great enthusiasm. Nevertheless, he set out and let the nets down.

The result of Peter's obedience was impressive. His nets filled up with so much fish that his nets began to break. Partners in the other boat were signaled to come out and help. Both boats were filled to where they began to overload. The catch was so great that Peter and his companions were totally amazed. I'm sure in all their days of fishing in the Sea of Galilee that they never had a catch like this.

Many of us know this story from the Book of Luke, but there's a simple point to be made. Peter was obedient, and as a result, was rewarded. Obedience is important to God. One may say that Jesus simply repaid Peter for the loan of his boat that He used for a temporary pulpit, but one must remember Peter was obedient to the Lord's request. Obedience to the Bible and its promises brings rewards. Obedience to the Holy Spirit and the call of God on our lives brings rewards. Isaiah 1:19 says, "If you consent and obey, you will eat the best of the land." Being willing and obedient to the Lord will bring us prosperous lives.

Let's look at a fictitious scenario that easily could be real. Let's say there's an inexperienced young pilot experiencing difficulties while flying in a storm and needs some guidance for landing safety. An exceptionally capable pilot from the Air Traffic Control station begins to give the young pilot definitive instructions. The young pilot complies with those instructions, and as a result, lands the plane safely. Equally, obedience to the Lord will bring us through the storms of life to safe ground. Many hazards in life can be avoided as we follow His voice. "Trust in the Lord with all your heart and do not lean on your own understanding. In all your ways acknowledge Him and He will make your paths straight." (Proverbs 3:5–6).

30

Guard Against Greed

The Lord warns against greed in the Bible. He uses a parable in Chapter 12 of Luke to explain that a man's life does not consist in the abundance of his possessions. A rich man is used as the character in the Lord's story.

The man was a rich farmer. His ground produced an abundance from his crops. He had more than enough and pondered what to do with all his extra grain and foodstuffs. He finally decides to tear down his barns and build bigger ones for extra storage. Thinking he had plenty stored up for many years, he decides to take life easy and eat, drink and be merry. The rich man was exceptionally content; however, God told him that that very night his life would end and asked him who would get all this storage that he had prepared for himself. The man was rich by worldly standards but not rich toward God.

I'm reminded of a story about a stingy rich man that peered out his window and saw people in need all around him. He then looked into an old mirror that was really only glass with a silver coating. He suddenly realized when the silver was added that he saw only himself.

When people die they leave all their material possessions. They can't take material possessions with them. No matter what is left, great or small, it can't be taken. One needs to be conscious of this and keep one's priorities in order. It takes money and goods to live and the Lord knows that. As one comes to Him, He'll meet those needs. "But seek first His kingdom and His righteousness, and all these things will be given to you as well." (Matthew 6:33). "Set your minds on things above, not on earthly things." (Colossians 3:2).

Let me say that the Lord wants to bless us. "Beloved, I pray that in all respects you may prosper and be in good health, just as your soul prospers." (III John 2). "The Lord be magnified, Who delights in the prosperity of His servant." (Psalm 35:27). God wants us to live prosperous lives but to be free from greed or covetousness. Jesus said to them, "Beware, and be on your guard against every form of greed; for not even when one has an abundance does his life consist of his possessions." (Luke 12:15).

If we live for this world, we will surely go out without anything, but if we live for the next one we will bless others on the way and depart the better for it.

31

Mary And Zacharias

Mary and Zacharias both had interesting experiences with God but with different results. One's voice was silenced for a season and one's life was immediately blessed.

Gabriel appeared to Zacharias while Zacharias was standing in the temple next to the altar of incense. The angel told Zacharias not to be afraid and that his wife Elizabeth would bear a son. The son would be called John and serve as a forerunner for the Lord. Zacharias questioned the angel with doubt since he and his wife were up in years. As a result, the angel took away his voice until these things would be fulfilled.

Gabriel also visited Mary. The angel told Mary that she had found favor with God and that she would bear a son. She would call the son Jesus. He would be great and called the Son of the Most High. Mary questioned the angel on how this could be since she was a virgin. It wasn't a statement of doubt and unbelief but one of a sincere and legitimate question since she had not known a man. Gabriel told Mary that the Holy Spirit would come upon her. Mary then came into complete agreement.

Zacharias basically asked for a sign or he wouldn't believe. Mary acquiesced to the will of God. Even though Zacharias and Elizabeth had prayed for a son, Zacharias staggered at this promise of God personally delivered by an angel. The Bible is full of wonderful promises but so many times they are met with unbelief and doubt in the lives of Christians. Christians pray and then they doubt even though they have the promises of God right before their eyes. Those promises are as real as if Gabriel was personally delivering them from the Lord. Mary stated, "Behold, the bondslave of the Lord; be it done according to your word." (Luke 1:38). Christians need to line up in agreement with God's Word and look for things to happen.

Doubt and unbelief rob people of blessings from God. Get in agreement like Mary, shun doubt and unbelief and look for God to honor His Word. "For as many as may be the promises of God, in Him they are yes; wherefore also by Him is our Amen to the glory of God through us." (II Corinthians 1:20). All the promises of God are "Yes" and "Amen" in Christ.

32
Wisdom Is A Choice

Solomon, shortly after his father David's death, established himself securely over his kingdom. He then proceeded to go up to the bronze altar which was at the tent of meeting and offered a thousand burnt offerings on it to the Lord. During that night God appeared to Solomon and asked him what God should give him. Solomon asked for wisdom and knowledge so that he could rule well over God's people. God was pleased over Solomon's response and granted him his request along with great riches, honor and wealth.

Much is said about wisdom in the Bible, especially in the Book of Proverbs. Wisdom can probably best be summarized as knowledge of God's Word and application of it in our daily lives. A wise man in God's eyes will always be one who knows the Word and applies it to all facets of his life. Solomon knew the importance of godly wisdom and a right relationship with God.

Many people in today's world think they're wise but they are not. Many pursue their lives through primarily carnal eyes and govern their actions by worldly and conventional wisdom. The ways of the world and its system are at variance with the ways of God. People proclaimed to be wise by human perceptions include tyrants, governmental leaders, successful businessmen, outstanding athletes and numerous others; however, many of them are not in God's eyes. Worldly wisdom without God severely lacks. The fear of the Lord or reverence of God is the starting point and essence of wisdom. No matter who he is, wealthy or poor, a man without God is not very wise.

Wisdom can only be obtained through a personal relationship with God. It starts with salvation and progresses from that point. Wisdom is not received in some mechanical way but must be developed. A man becomes wiser as he nurtures and applies God's Word in his life. "The fear of the Lord is the beginning of wisdom; A good understanding have all those who do His commandments; His praise endures forever." (Psalm 11:10). "The fear of the Lord is the beginning of knowledge; Fools despise wisdom and instruction." (Proverbs 1:7). Let us become wise in God's sight by becoming knowledgeable of His Word and applying it in our lives.

33

Mary Chose Well

The disciples were traveling along when they entered Bethany. A woman named Martha welcomed Jesus into her home. She quickly became busy with much preparations while her sister, Mary, sat at the Lord's feet. Jesus preached the gospel wherever He went and Mary was resolved to receive all that she could from the Master's words.

Martha was cumbered about with much serving and that was the reason why she was not where Mary was. Martha's heart was wrapped up with elaborate preparations. Entertaining the Lord was good on her part but her inordinate care of preparations was in excess. Martha protested to Jesus that Mary should help her but Jesus commended Mary for listening and basically told Martha that she was too worried and bothered with preparations. Perhaps a simple dish would have sufficed vice what Martha was trying to prepare. This would have allowed her more time with Jesus.

Inordinate care over worldly activities will affect one's walk and time with the Lord. People can easily become entangled with excess concern over worldly affairs and of things that will pass away. Jesus makes it clear that Mary chose the better pursuit. It's important for us all to evaluate our schedules and allocation of time towards worldly activities in light of time with the Lord. The contrast of Mary and Martha in this situation provides an interesting lesson for us all.

It's clear that Mary had her priorities in order while Martha was entangled over an excess concern that took quality time away from the Lord. Mary chose well. She truly wanted to develop in the things of God. To do that, it takes time with Him. You won't develop in the things of God through any other way. "You shall follow the Lord your God and fear Him; and you shall keep His commandments, listen to His voice, serve Him, and cling to Him." (Deuteronomy 13:4). "I urge you therefore, brethren, by the mercies of God, to present your bodies a living and holy sacrifice, acceptable to God, which is your spiritual service of worship. And do not be conformed to this world, but be transformed by the renewing of your mind, that you may prove what the will of God is, that which is good and acceptable and perfect." (Romans 12:1–2).

34

Be Quick To Repent

The time was approaching when Jesus would go to the cross. He continued to try and prepare His disciples for things to come. As He was discussing His departure, Peter became very inquisitive. Peter stated that he would lay down his life for Jesus. Jesus then stated that Peter would deny him three times before the cock would crow that evening.

Later in the evening Jesus was arrested in the Garden of Gethsemane and led away. Peter followed at a distance, and subsequently, due to his fear of man, denied the Lord during three separate and distinct instances. The Lord looked at Peter shortly after the cock crowed and Peter went out and wept bitterly. Peter suddenly realized that he had denied Jesus three times just as the Lord told him he would.

Even though Peter disowned and failed the Lord during this sequence of events, it is important to realize that Peter later repented, believed and was pardoned. You may recall, that although Judas Iscariot showed remorse for his betrayal of Jesus, he never came back to the Lord to seek reconciliation before he hanged himself. Many people come to the Lord and later backslide. Christians make mistakes and some may occasionally wander, but God forgives those that will repent and come back to Him. Never lose sight of this.

The Lord says He will never leave or forsake you when you come to Him. Jesus is compassionately concerned over our misguided actions and deeds. Peter disowned Jesus, but Jesus did not disown Peter. Christ doesn't deal with man the way man deals with Him. The Lord's eyes were already guiding and ministering to Peter when He looked at Peter after Peter's denials. The Lord's eyes did not verbally speak but they appealed with direction and compassion. That look had immediate impact on Peter's life and helped lead Peter to repentance. Eventually, Peter would become a great man of God.

If you're a backslidden Christian, Jesus wants you to know that He'll forgive you. He wants restoration because He loves you so much. Those inner tuggings are Christ looking at and appealing to you to get back on course. "And the Lord turned and looked at Peter. And Peter remembered the word of the Lord, how He had told him, Before a cock crows today, you will deny Me three times. And he went out and wept bitterly." (Luke 22:61–62). A compassionate Jesus is looking at us today. Be quick to repent and go forward in God. It's in our best interest.

35
The Penitent Thief

This final section takes us to the scene of the crucifixion. The rulers and soldiers were sarcastically mocking and insulting Jesus as He hung on the cross. Jesus was also surrounded by two thieves who were being crucified next to Him. One of the thieves joined in the abuse towards Jesus but the other thief took a different and more correct course of action.

The actions taken by the second thief in the last few minutes of his life brought him into Paradise. What a wise decision. The second thief rebuked the thief that was verbally abusing Jesus and then came to Jesus with a penitent heart just before he was to die. Jesus said unto the penitent thief, "Truly I say to you, today you shall be with Me in Paradise." (Luke 22:43). It would have been so easy for the penitent thief to have joined in the mockery but something gripped his heart with the truth. He realized deity was in his midst. He realized that he was guilty and deserved to be there but that Christ did not. He appealed to Jesus in faith and Jesus answered his petition with great favor.

The Lord always has an open ear to the penitent heart. The crucifixion was a moment of great agony and struggle for Jesus but He still had time and a comforting word for this penitent thief. Even the greatest of sinners can obtain pardon through the blood of Jesus. Jesus died for all sinners. One may feel that their deeds are too great to be forgiven, but that's not so. The penitent thief shows us it's not too late to come to Christ. It's important for all, while there is life, to come to Christ. Actions taken by the penitent thief allowed him entrance into Paradise. If he had not taken those steps before his death, it would not have been so. It's unfortunate the other thief did not do the same. Jesus said, "Truly, truly, I say to you, unless one is born again, he cannot see the kingdom of God." (John 3:3). "For God so loved the world, that He gave His only begotten Son, that whoever believes in Him should not perish, but have eternal life." (John 3:16).

Conclusion

These simple lessons will help us to live better lives as we apply them, but the most important biblical lesson and decision in a man's life is that of salvation. If there is any doubt as to your salvation, then I urge you to consider the following scriptures.

"As it is written, there is none righteous, not even one." (Romans 3:10).

"For all have sinned and fall short of the glory of God." (Romans 3:23).

"For the wages of sin is death, but the free gift of God is eternal life in Christ Jesus our Lord." (Romans 6:23).

"For there is one God, and one mediator also between God and men, the man Christ Jesus." (I Timothy 2:5).

"That if you confess with your mouth Jesus as Lord, and believe in your heart that God raised Him from the dead, you shall be saved; for with the heart man believes, resulting in righteousness, and with the mouth he confesses, resulting in salvation." (Romans 10:9–10).

Now, a Sinner's Prayer to receive Jesus as Lord and Savior. Please repeat the following prayer and mean it from your heart. You must be sincere or they will only be words, and mean nothing. If you are sincere, then God is sincere because God always honors His Word.

"Dear Heavenly Father, I come to You in the name of the Lord Jesus Christ. I ask you to forgive me of all my sins. I accept Jesus as my Lord and Savior and believe in my heart that He died on the cross for my sins and that You raised Him from the dead for my justification. I now repent and confess Jesus as my Lord and Savior. I thank You for saving me and ask that You would help me in my Christian walk."

I strongly encourage you to read your Bible daily to get to know the Lord better, talk to God daily in prayer and find a church where the Bible is taught as the complete Word of God. I also recommend that you be water baptized.

Footnotes

1. The Ryrie Study Bible. New American Standard Translation. Copyright 1976, 1978 by The Moody Bible Institute, Chicago, Illinois, page 47.

2. Ibid, page 410.

3. Ibid, page 596.

4. Ibid, page 712.

5. Ibid, pages 367 and 539.

6. Ibid, page 476.

About The Author

Commander Michael H. Imhof, U.S. Navy (ret.), was born in Fort Bragg, North Carolina and raised in Blasdell, New York. He attended the State University College of New York at Buffalo, where he received a Bachelor of Science degree. He was commissioned in 1973. After completing Basic Underwater Demolition/SEAL training in Coronado, California, Commander Imhof was assigned to SEAL Team TWO, and subsequent Naval Special Warfare and other type commands.

Commander Imhof, possessing a Naval Special Warfare designator, has served throughout the world in numerous positions. Assignments include Platoon Commander, Training Officer, Operations Officer, Staff Officer, Executive Officer and Commanding Officer. He also earned a Master's Degree in Administration from George Washington University and served as an instructor at the U.S. Naval Academy. His awards include Defense Meritorious Service Medal; Meritorious Service Medal with two Gold Stars in lieu of second and third awards; Joint Service Commendation Medal; Navy Commendation Medal with Gold Star in lieu of second award; United Nations Medal; and other service awards.

A military officer of strong Christian convictions, Commander Imhof is ready and willing to share his faith with all. He is convinced that the Bible is the authoritative and uncompromising Word of God and gives thanks for the wonderful blessings of God in his life and the lives of his family. He is an active member in his local church.

TEACH Services, Inc.
P U B L I S H I N G

We invite you to view the complete
selection of titles we publish at:
www.TEACHServices.com

We encourage you to write us
with your thoughts about this,
or any other book we publish at:
info@TEACHServices.com

TEACH Services' titles may be purchased in
bulk quantities for educational, fund-raising,
business, or promotional use.
bulksales@TEACHServices.com

Finally, if you are interested in seeing
your own book in print, please contact us at:
publishing@TEACHServices.com
We are happy to review your manuscript at no charge.

www.ingramcontent.com/pod-product-compliance
Lightning Source LLC
Chambersburg PA
CBHW060443090426
42733CB00011B/2372